VIOLINJUDY'S
A VIOLIN HALLOWEEN

SUPPLEMENTARY SONGS AND ACTIVITIES FOR BEGINNING THROUGH METHOD BOOK LEVEL 2 VIOLIN STUDENTS

VERY FUN VIOLIN COLLECTION

A Violin Halloween by Judy Naillon
Copyright © 2019 ViolinJudy
www.violinjudy.com
ISBN 978-1-960674-01-2

All Rights Reserved. This book or parts thereof may not be reproduced in any form, stored in any retrieval system, or transmitted in any form by any means-eletronic, mechanical, photocopy, recording, or otherwise - without prior written permission or the publisher, except as provided by copyright law.

VERY FUN VIOLIN LIBRARY

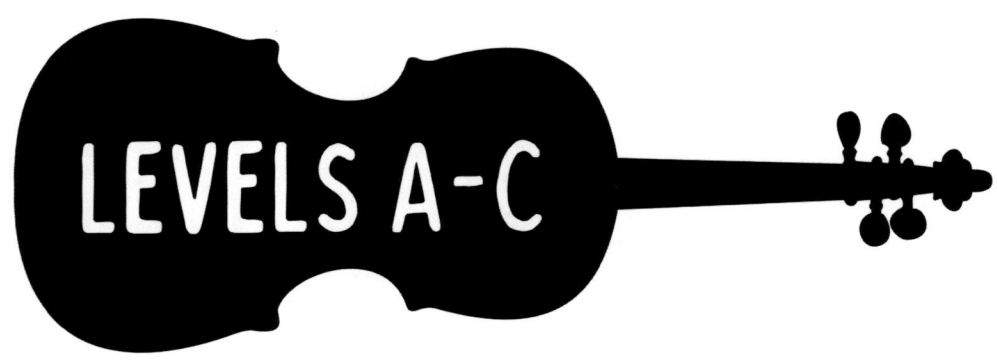

A *Violin Halloween* is composed for violin students in levels A-C. Children using this book should be able to hold the instrument up in playing position and understand a basic bow grip. A book level chart for the *Very Fun Violin Collection* is provided at the end of this book.

1. SAY BOO!
2. HALLOWEEN TALK
3. VERY SCARY RUNNING PUMPKINS
4. HALLOWEEN TIME
5. HOT CROSS BUNS
6. HALLOWEEN NIGHT
7. HALLOWEEN WALTZ
8. MY NEW COSTUME
9. HALLOWEEN PARTY
10. MAKE A JACK-O-LANTERN
11. STIR THE WITCHES` BREW
12. TRICK OR TREAT
13. HOT "CROSS" BUNS
14. ACCIDENTALS
15. DANCING PUMPKINHEADS
17. LITTLE GHOST
19. CHOPIN`S HALLOWEEN
21. THE PINK GHOST
23. SPOOKY
25. LEARN TREMOLO
26. 5 LITTLE PUMPKINS
27. GHOST OF JOHN

SAY BOO!

FLY OFF THE STRING AND CIRCLE BACK TO THE FROG AT THE END OF EACH LINE!

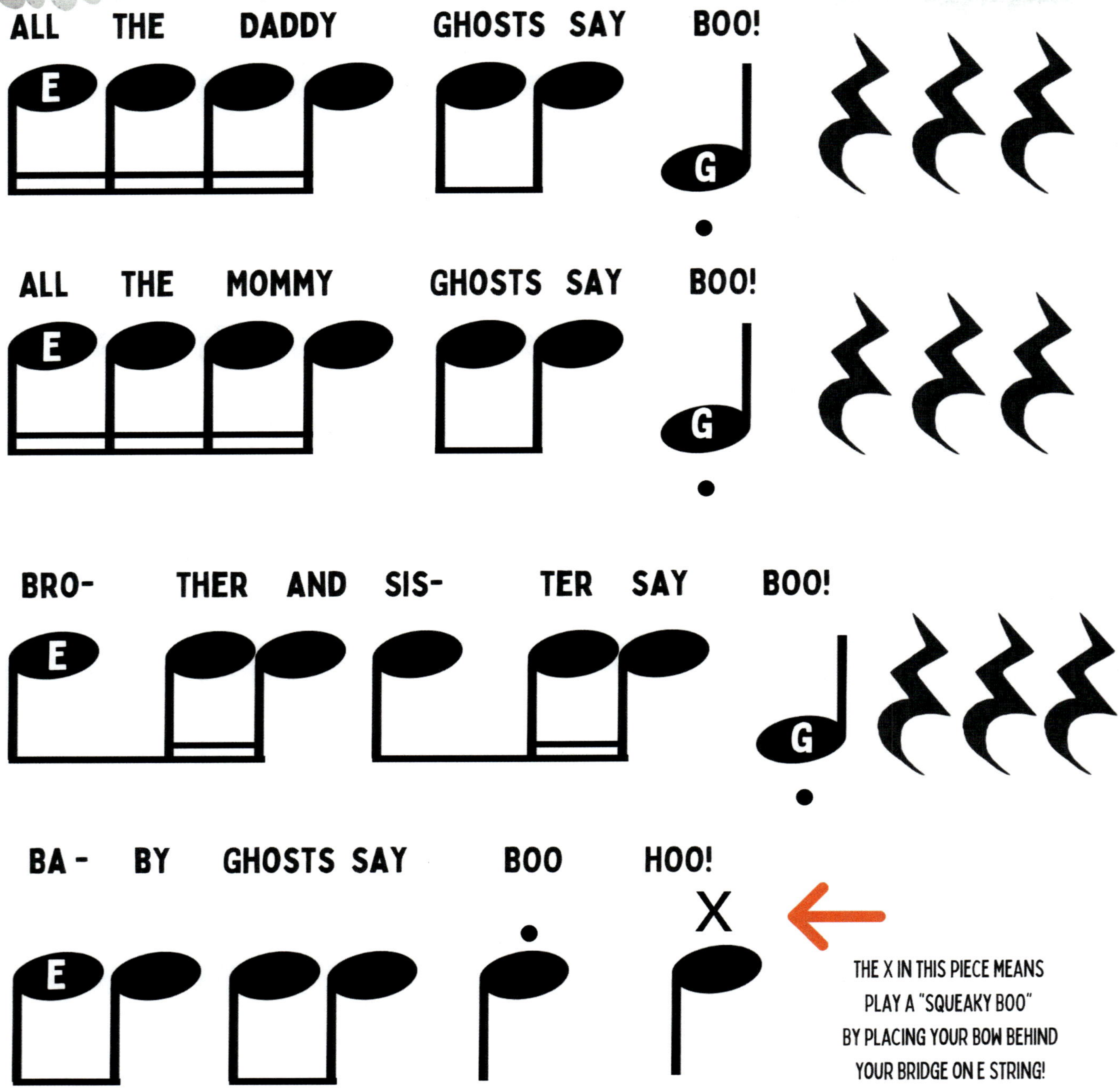

ALL THE DADDY GHOSTS SAY BOO!

ALL THE MOMMY GHOSTS SAY BOO!

BRO- THER AND SIS- TER SAY BOO!

BA- BY GHOSTS SAY BOO HOO!

THE X IN THIS PIECE MEANS PLAY A "SQUEAKY BOO" BY PLACING YOUR BOW BEHIND YOUR BRIDGE ON E STRING! IT WILL SOUND LIKE THE BABY GHOST CRYING!

C. JUDY NAILLON 2019 WWW.VIOLINJUDY.COM

A VIOLIN HALLOWEEN P.1

HALLOWEEN TALK

FLY OFF THE STRING AT THE END OF LINE ONE.
DO YOU RECOGNIZE THESE RHYTHMS FROM OTHER SONGS YOU HAVE LEARNED?

THIS IS WHAT WE SAY ON HALLO - WEEN

E   A

CAN - DY,   PLEASE, AND   THANK YOU,

A

TRICK - OR -   TREAT,   SMELL   MY   FEET,

D

GIVE   ME   SOME-THING   GOOD   TO   EAT!

G

C. JUDY NAILLON 2019 WWW.VIOLINJUDY.COM   A VIOLIN HALLOWEEN P.2

HALLOWEEN TIME

THIS PIECE WILL HELP YOU LEARN DOWN AND UP BOWS.
START ON E STRING THEN TRY THIS PIECE ON A, D AND G STRING.
USE BIG WHOLE BOWS FOR EACH NOTE.
AFTER YOU HAVE LEARNED THIS PIECE ON OPEN STRINGS,
ADD FINGERS TO COMPOSE YOUR OWN PIECE!

HAL - LO - WEEN IS HERE, MY

FLY OFF THE STRING AND
CIRCLE BACK TO THE FROG

FAV - ORITE TIME OF YEAR.

WE SAY "TRICK - OR - TREAT" AND

GET GOOD THINGS TO EAT!

C. JUDY NAILLON 2019 WWW.VIOLINJUDY.COM   A VIOLIN HALLOWEEN P.4

HOT CROSS BUNS

THIS PIECE HAS FINGER 2 SNUGGLED UP NEXT TO FINGER 1 ON E STRING!

THIS SONG IS REALLY FUN, SO YOU CAN REPEAT IT THREE MORE TIMES USING A, D, THEN G STRING.

HALLOWEEN NIGHT
A PIECE TO PRACTICE GETTING TO THE FROG!

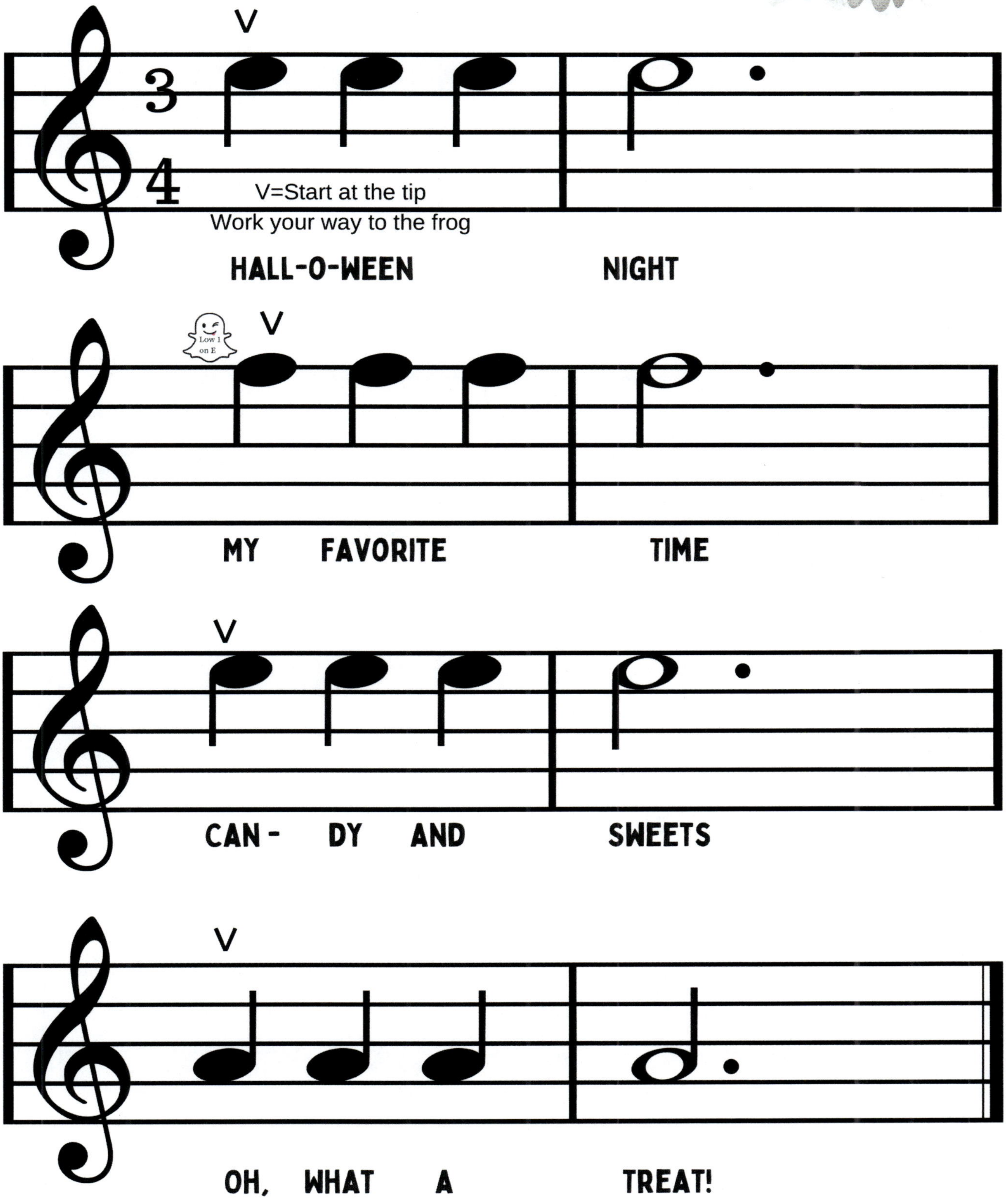

V=Start at the tip
Work your way to the frog

HALL-O-WEEN NIGHT

MY FAVORITE TIME

CAN- DY AND SWEETS

OH, WHAT A TREAT!

A HALLOWEEN WALTZ
A PIECE TO PRACTICE GETTING TO THE TIP!

A VIOLIN HALLOWEEN P.7

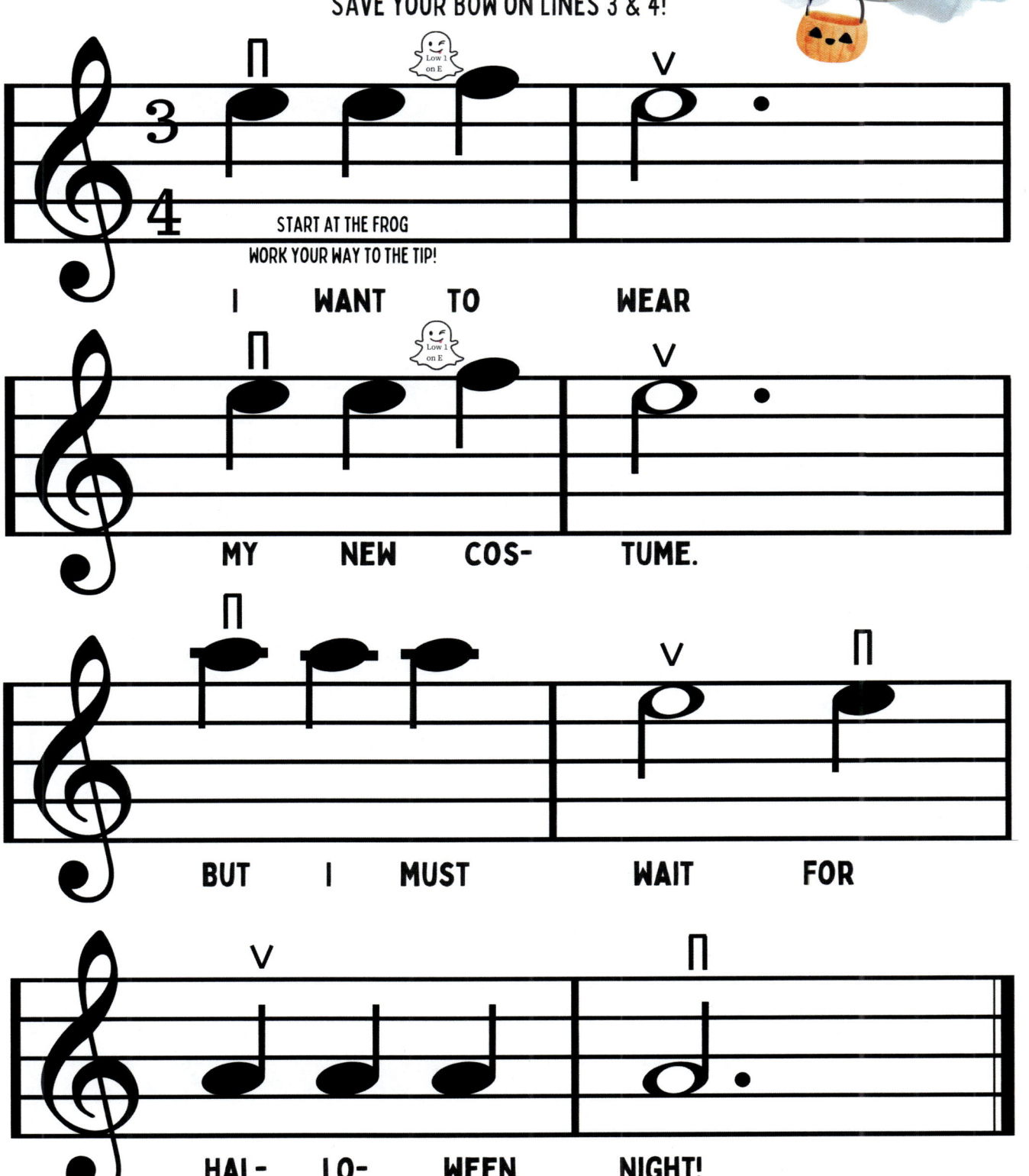

HALLOWEEN PARTY
A PIECE TO PRACTICE GETTING TO THE TIP!

MAKE A JACK-O-LANTERN
A PIECE TO PRACTICE LIFTING AND CIRCLING BACK!

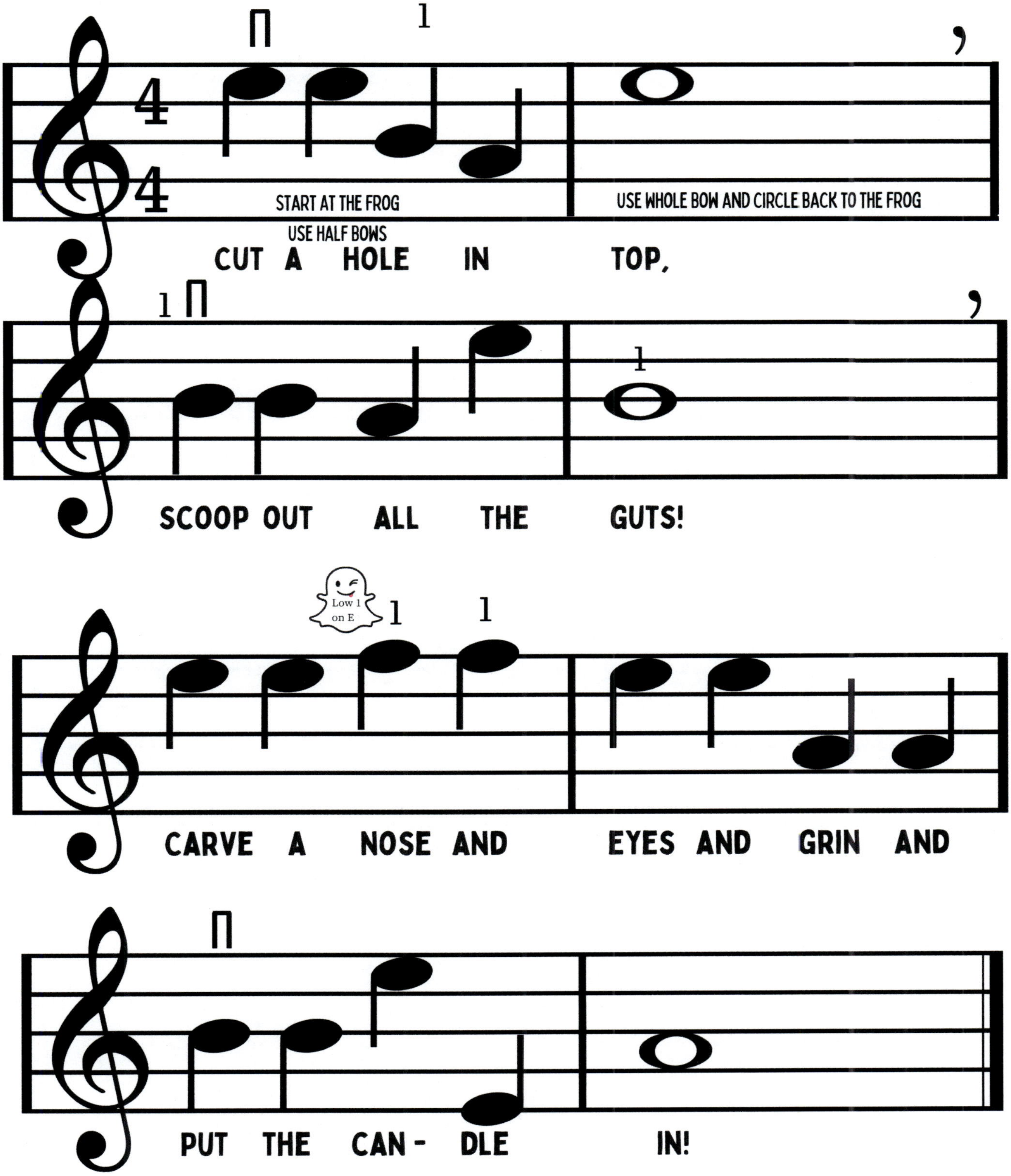

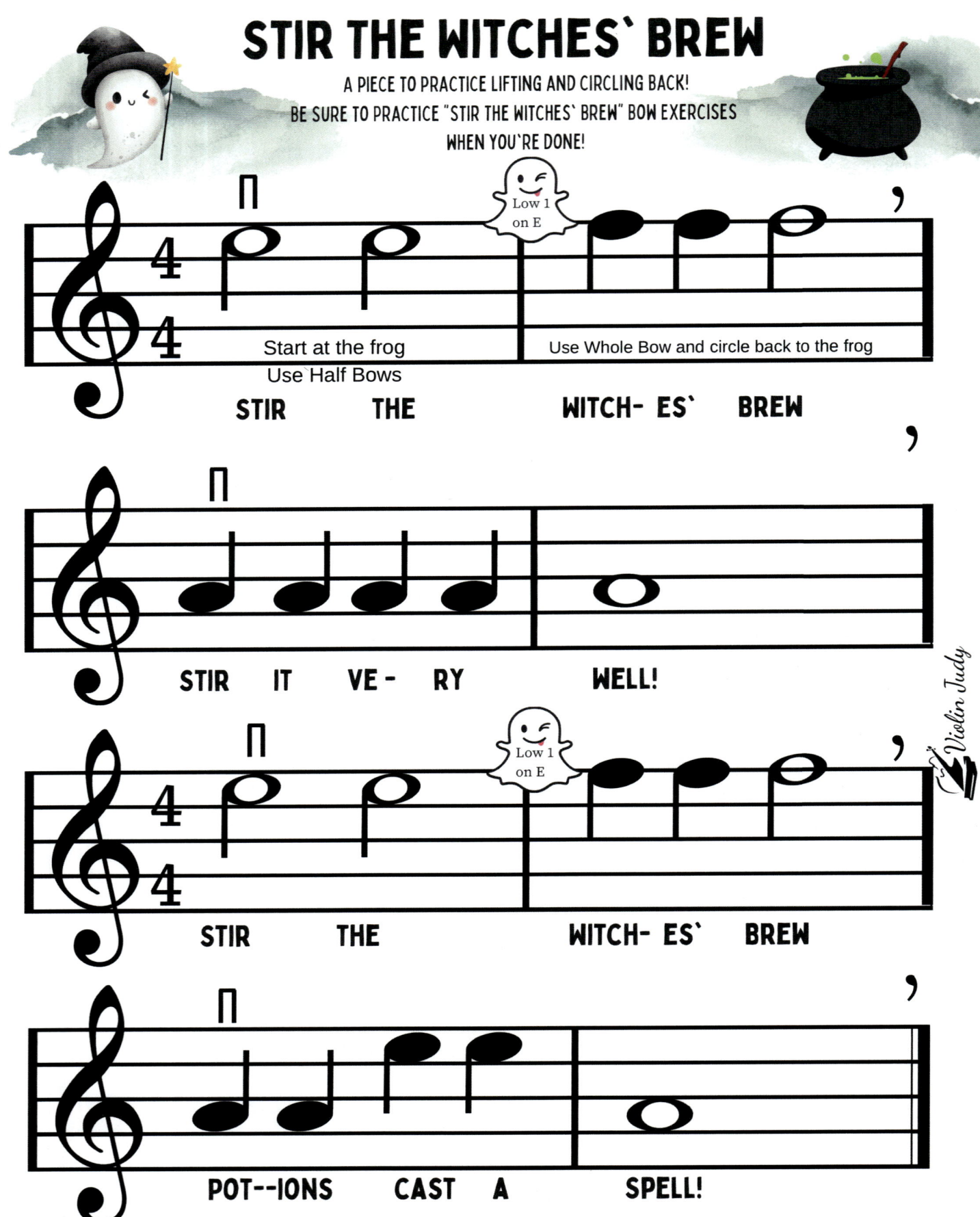

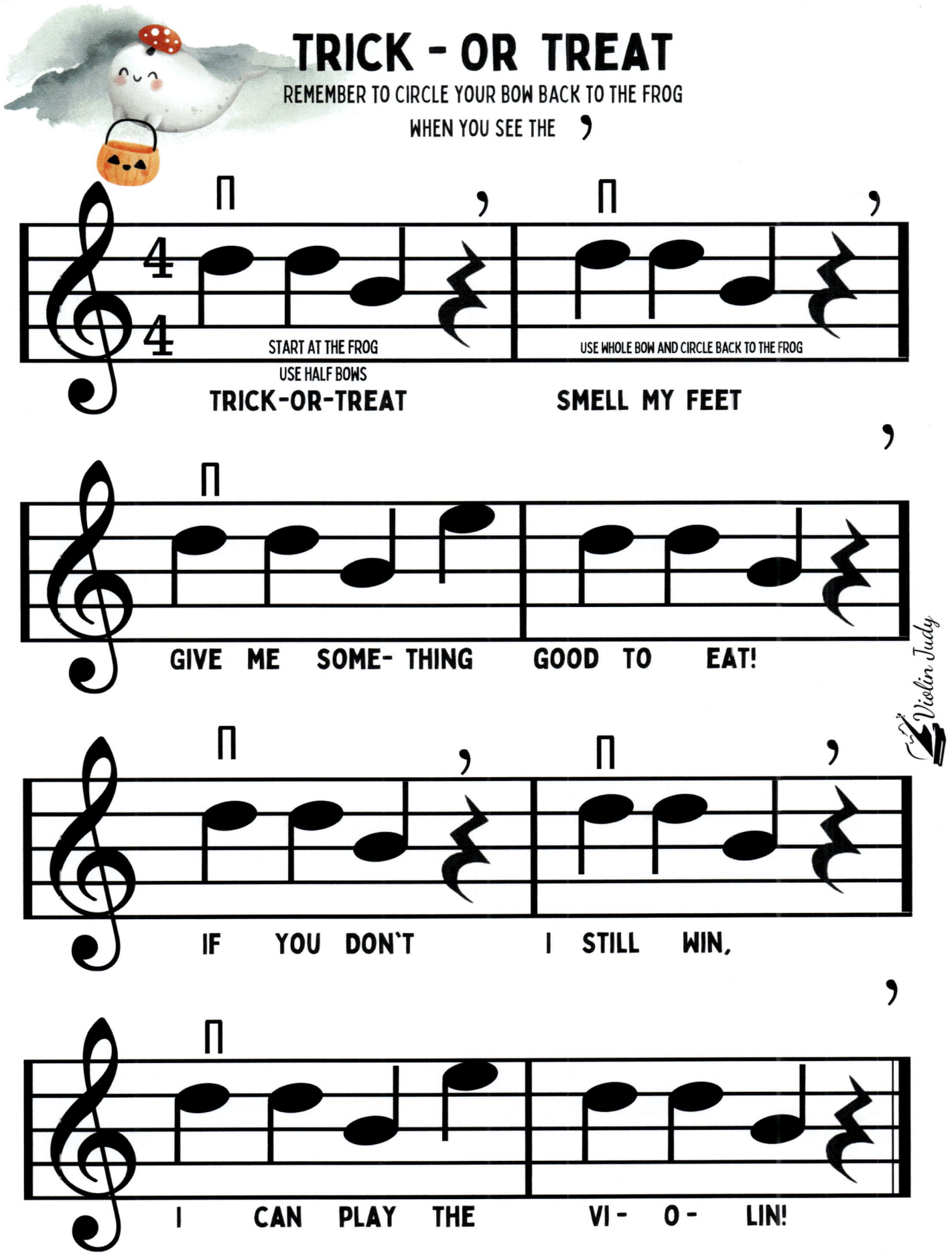

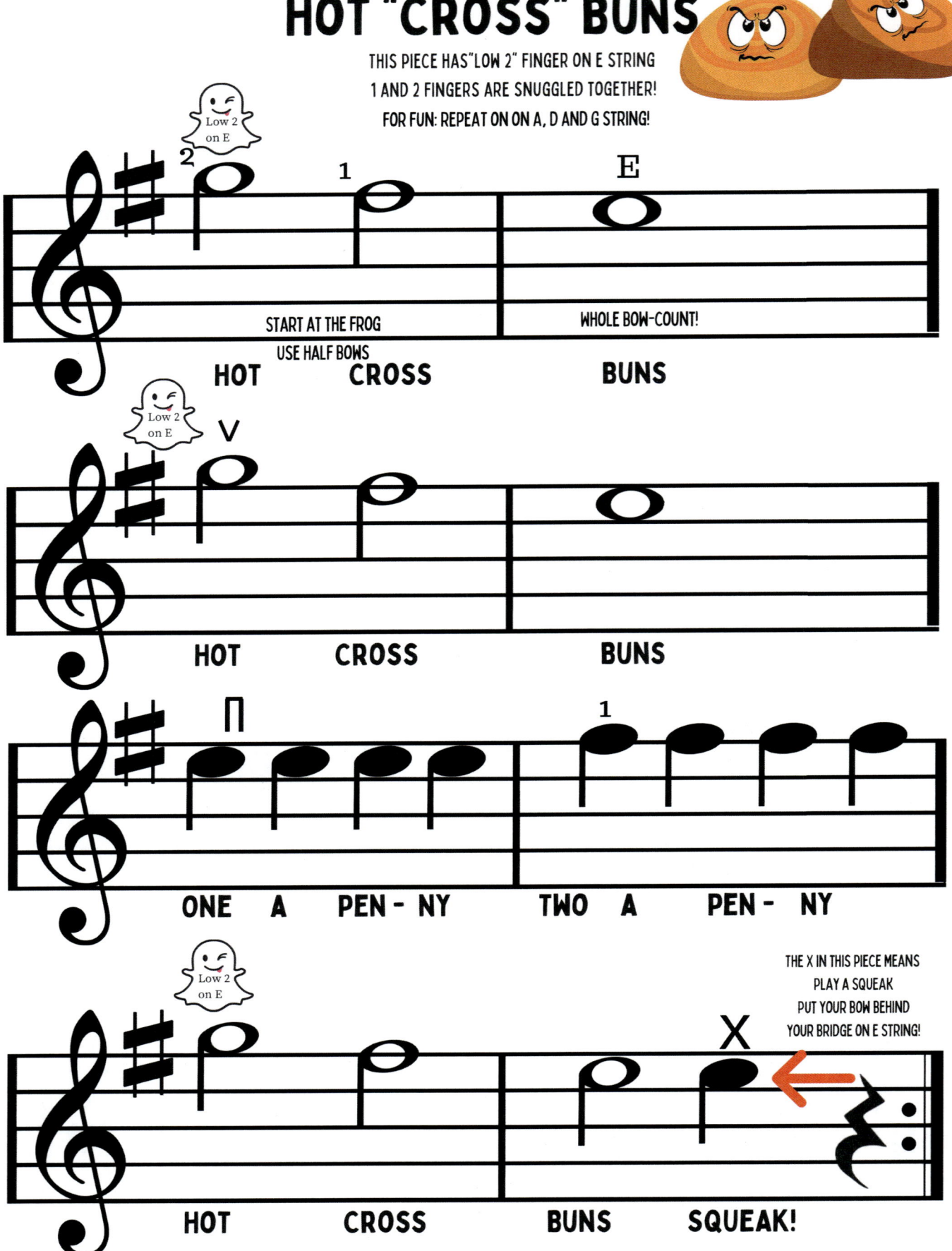

ACCIDENTALS

♭ FLAT   **♯ SHARP**   **♮ NATURAL**

Music has a lot of secret codes that do not have directions or any way to know the rules written in the music.
This can be very confusing but the more you practice the better you'll get!
Here is a rule about accidentals that is VERY important.
If a note has an accidental in front of the note it will stay that way the entire measure.
So if we have a note like F sharp in measure one, the sharp is only written once. All the notes of the same pitch (F) will be sharp
until the measure ends with a bar line. The bar line is like a magic eraser for accidentals! To help you remember this rule there
are erasers on the bar lines on lines 1 and 2.
You'll need to remember that bar lines erase sharps on line three and in the future in everything you play.
Natural signs can always cancel sharps and flats. We will practice this more in *A Twinkle Book C*
Sharps flats, and naturals are ALL accidentals.
Once a note has been changed to a sharp or flat, it stays that way for the whole measure.
The sharp or flat sign is not written again in the same measure.

IN THE BLUE BOX WRITE THE NUMBER OF ACCIDENTALS IN EACH MEASURE.

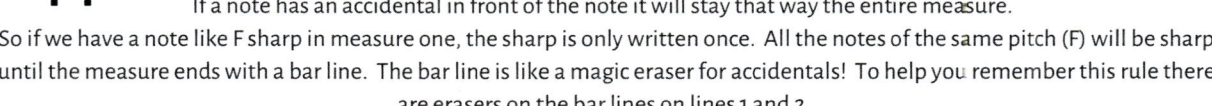

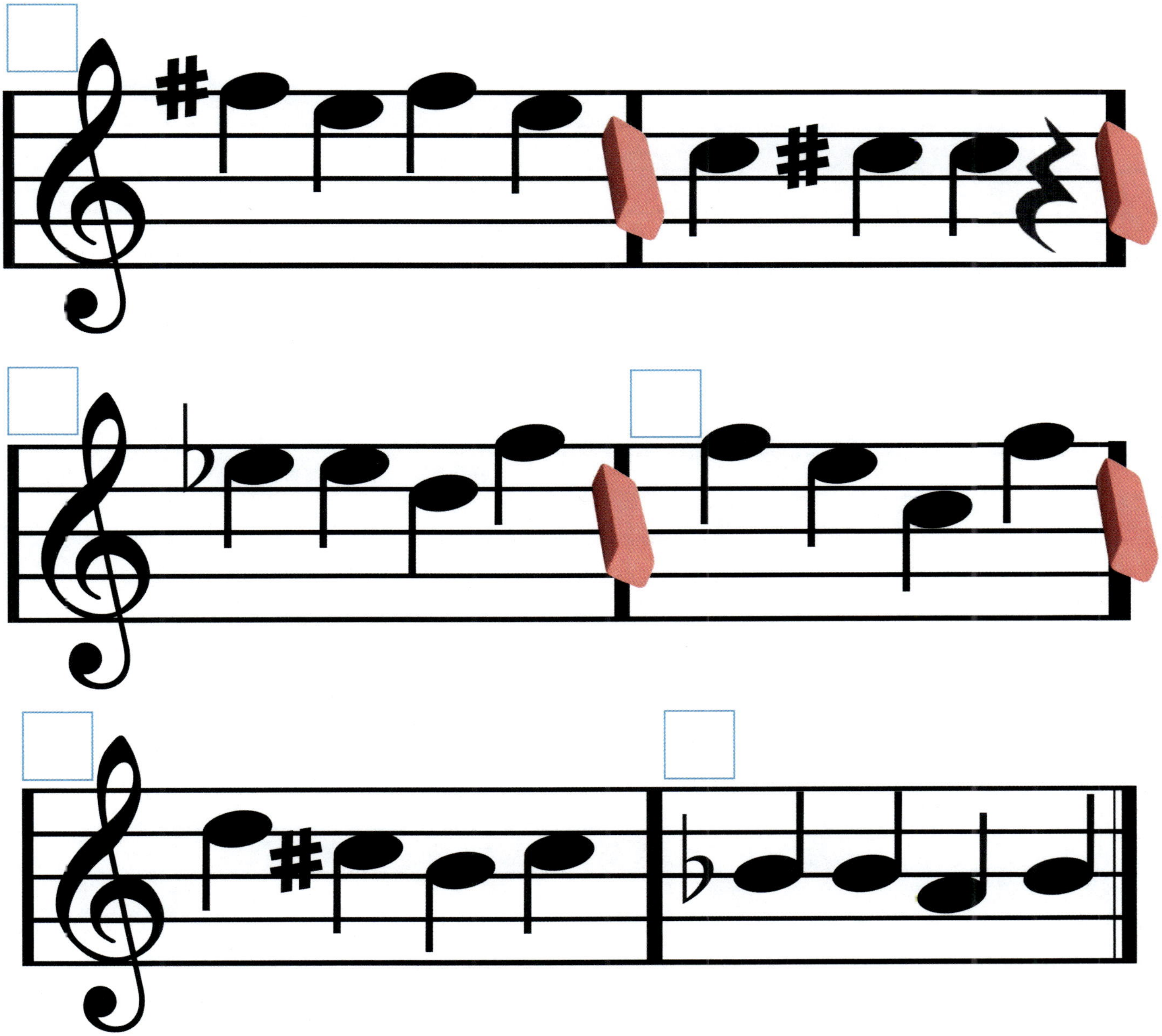

DANCING WITH THE PUMPKIN HEADS

THIS PIECE HAS "LOW 2" FINGER ON A STRING
1 AND 2 FINGERS ARE SNUGGLED TOGETHER!

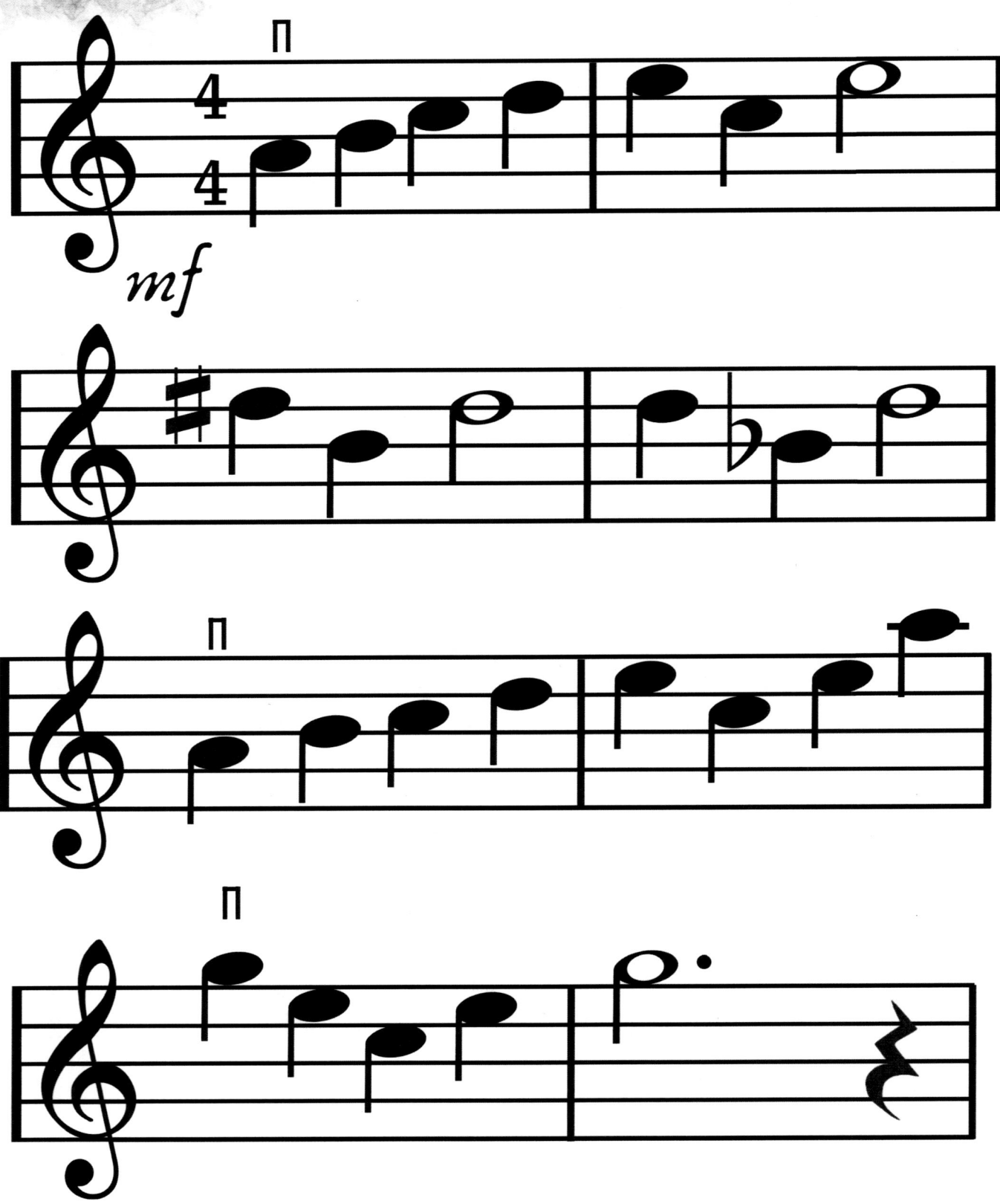

Dancing with the Pumpkin Heads

THE LITTLE GHOST

THIS PIECE HAS "LOW 2" FINGER ON A STRING
1 AND 2 FINGERS ARE SNUGGLED TOGETHER!

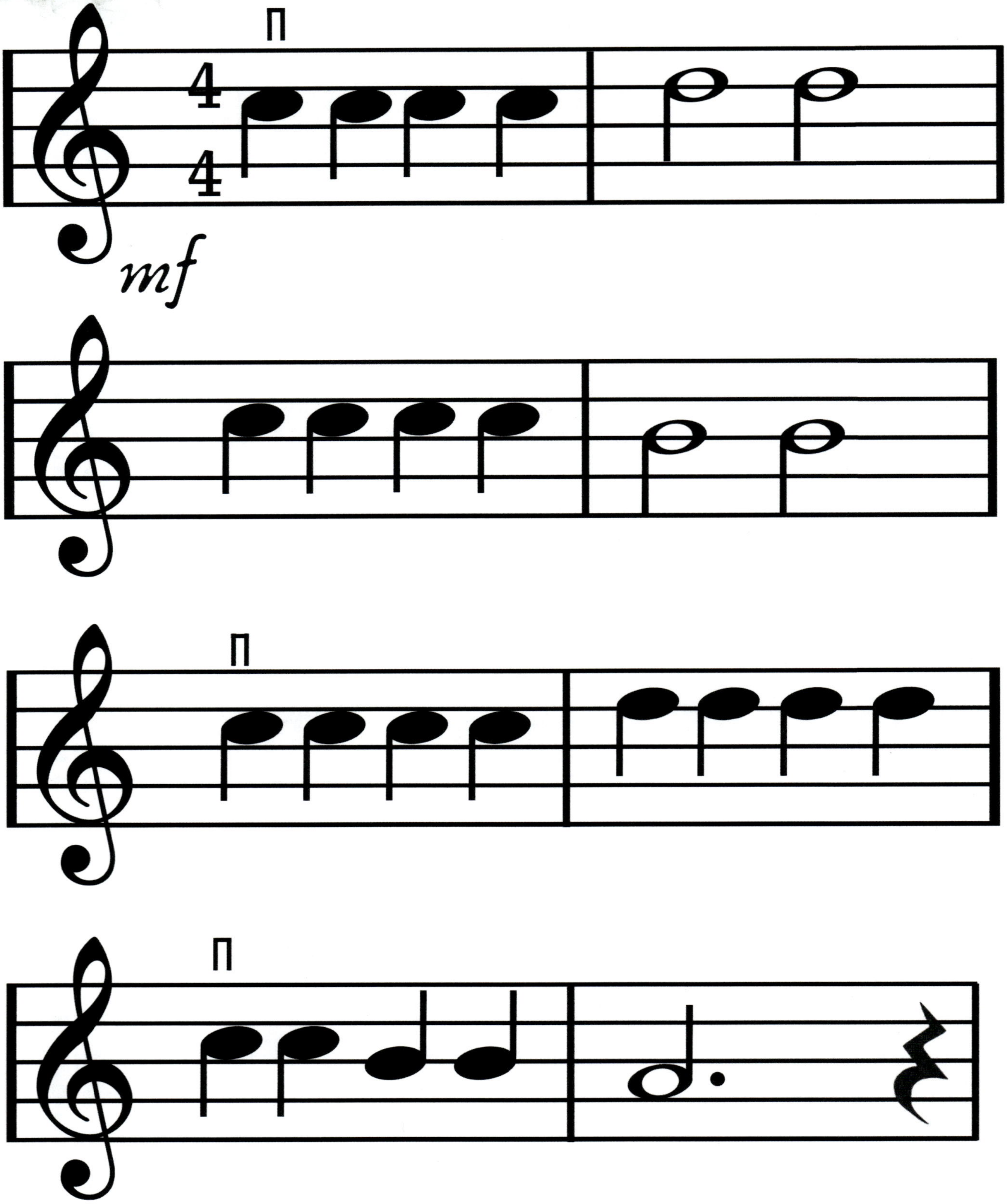

mf

WHY DO YOU THINK THE GHOST IS SAD?

THE LITTLE GHOST

A VIOLIN HALLOWEEN P.18

CHOPIN'S HALLOWEEN
THIS PIECE HAS "LOW 2" FINGER ON G & D STRING

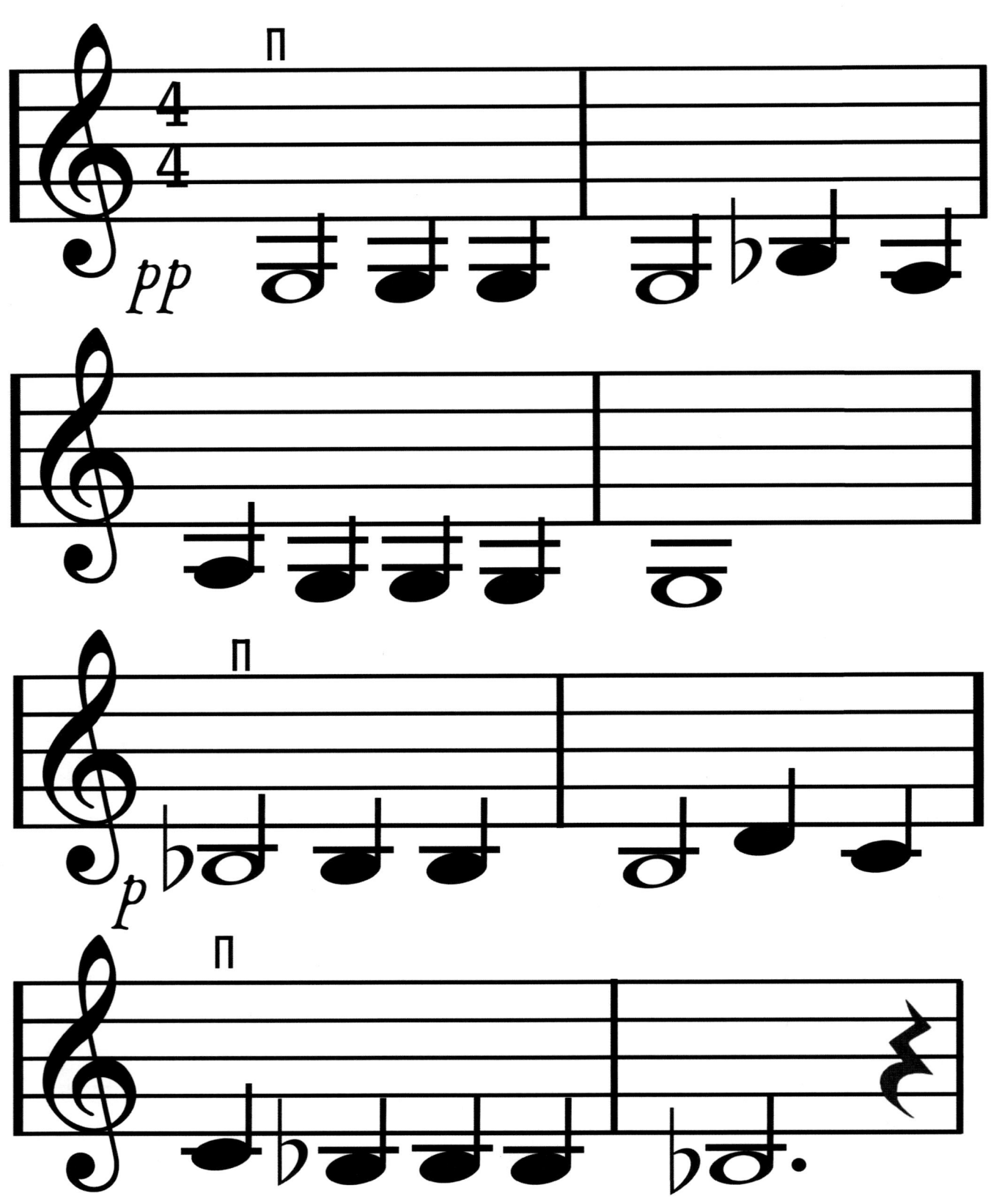

CHOPIN`S HALLOWEEN

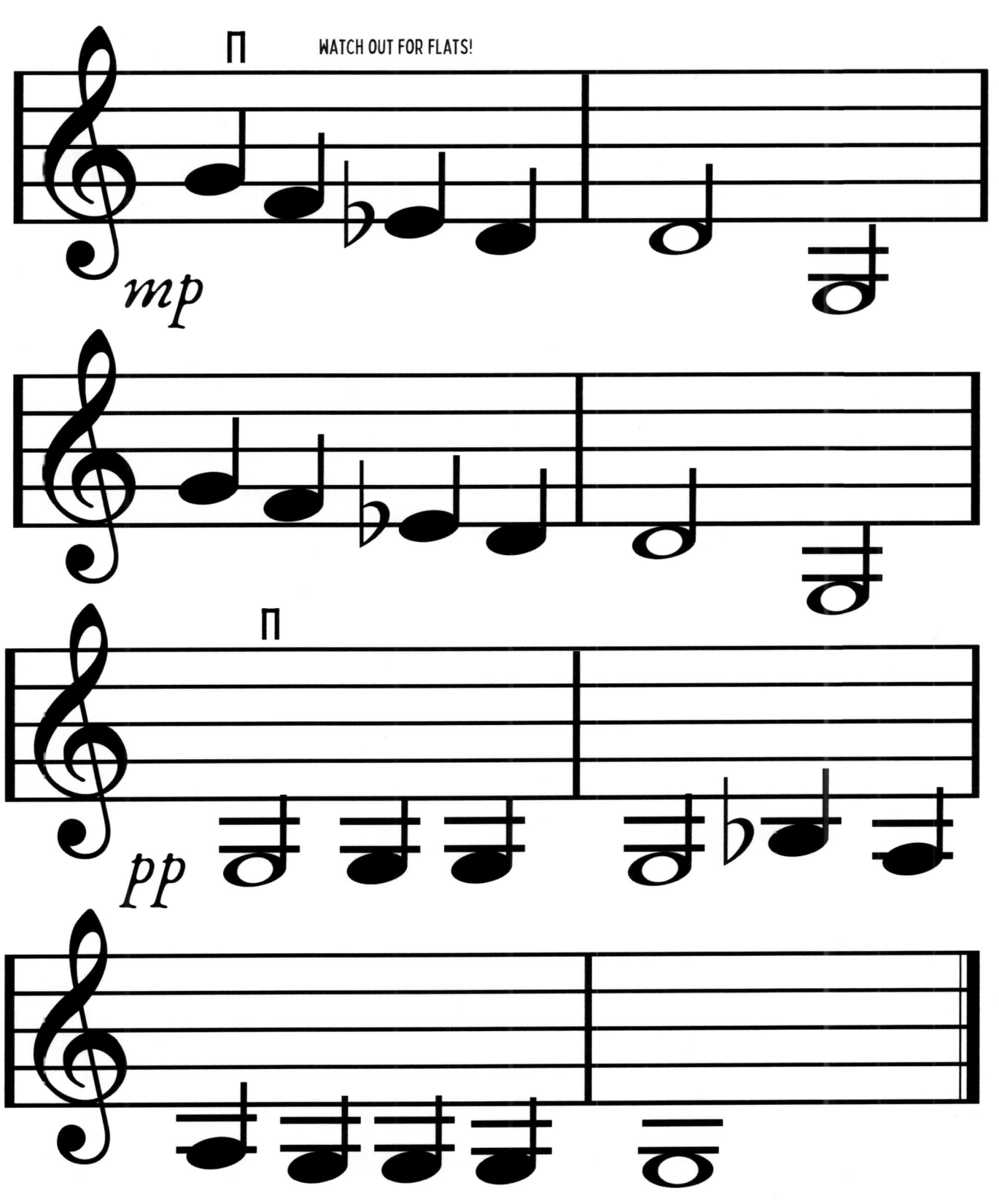

A VIOLIN HALLOWEEN P.20

THE PINK GHOST

THE PICTURES IN THIS SONG TELL A STORY OF A GHOST WHO DYED HERSELF PINK.
CAN YOU USE THE PICTURES TO TELL THE REST OF THE STORY?

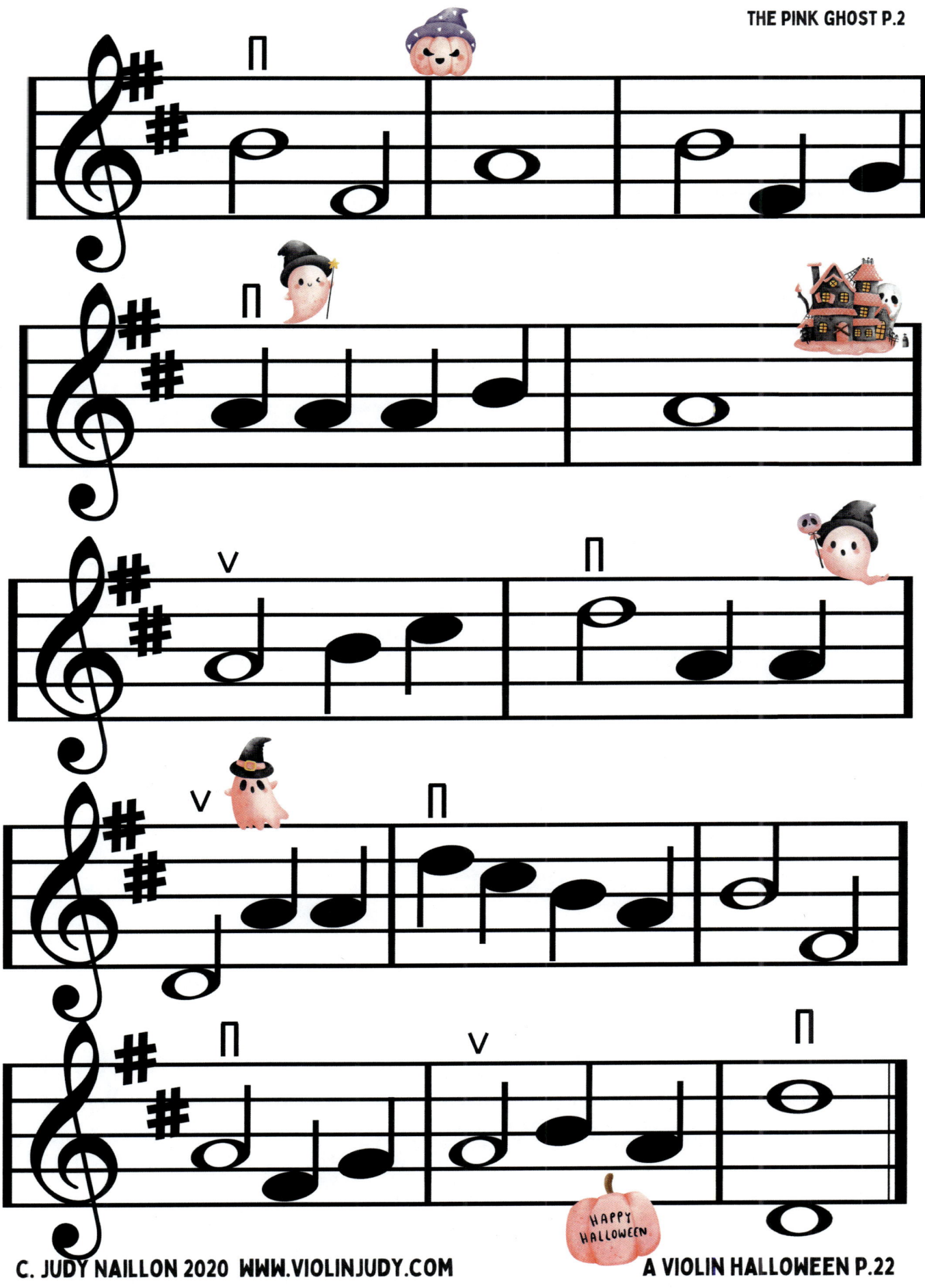

SPOOKY

A VIOLIN HALLOWEEN P.23

SPOOKY

A VIOLIN HALLOWEEN P.24

LET'S LEARN: TREMOLO

A TREMOLO IS A SPECIAL BOW EFFECT VIOLINISTS CAN USE. TREMOLO MEANS TREMBLING. THINK ABOUT SHIVERING WHEN YOU ARE COLD OR SCARED! YOU CAN MAKE YOUR BOW ARM MOVE VERY FAST WHILE USING A SMALL AMOUNT OF BOW TO CREATE A TREMOLO SOUND. DON'T WORRY IF YOUR FIRST TRIES SEEM TOO SLOW, AS YOU PRACTICE THESE COOL SOUND EFFECTS YOUR BOW ARM WILL GET FASTER AND FASTER! I TELL MY STUDENTS TO PRETEND YOUR BOW IS AN ELECTRIC TOOTHBRUSH!

FUN FACT: THE TREMOLO WAS INVENTED IN 1624 BY CLAUDIO MONTEVERDI

LOOK FOR THE THREE LINES OVER OR UNDER NOTE HEADS- THIS IS THE SECRET CODE OF VIOLINISTS FOR TREMOLO!

PRO TIP: I LIKE TO USE THE UPPER HALF OF MY BOW TO PLAY THE WHOLE NOTE TREMOLOS IN THE NEXT PIECE

REMEMBER: A TREMOLO IS NOT A TRILL. YOU DON'T NEED TO CHANGE THE PITCH (YOUR FINGERS ON THE VIOLIN)
THE ONLY THING THAT CHANGES IS YOUR BOW SPEED!

THE GHOST OF JOHN

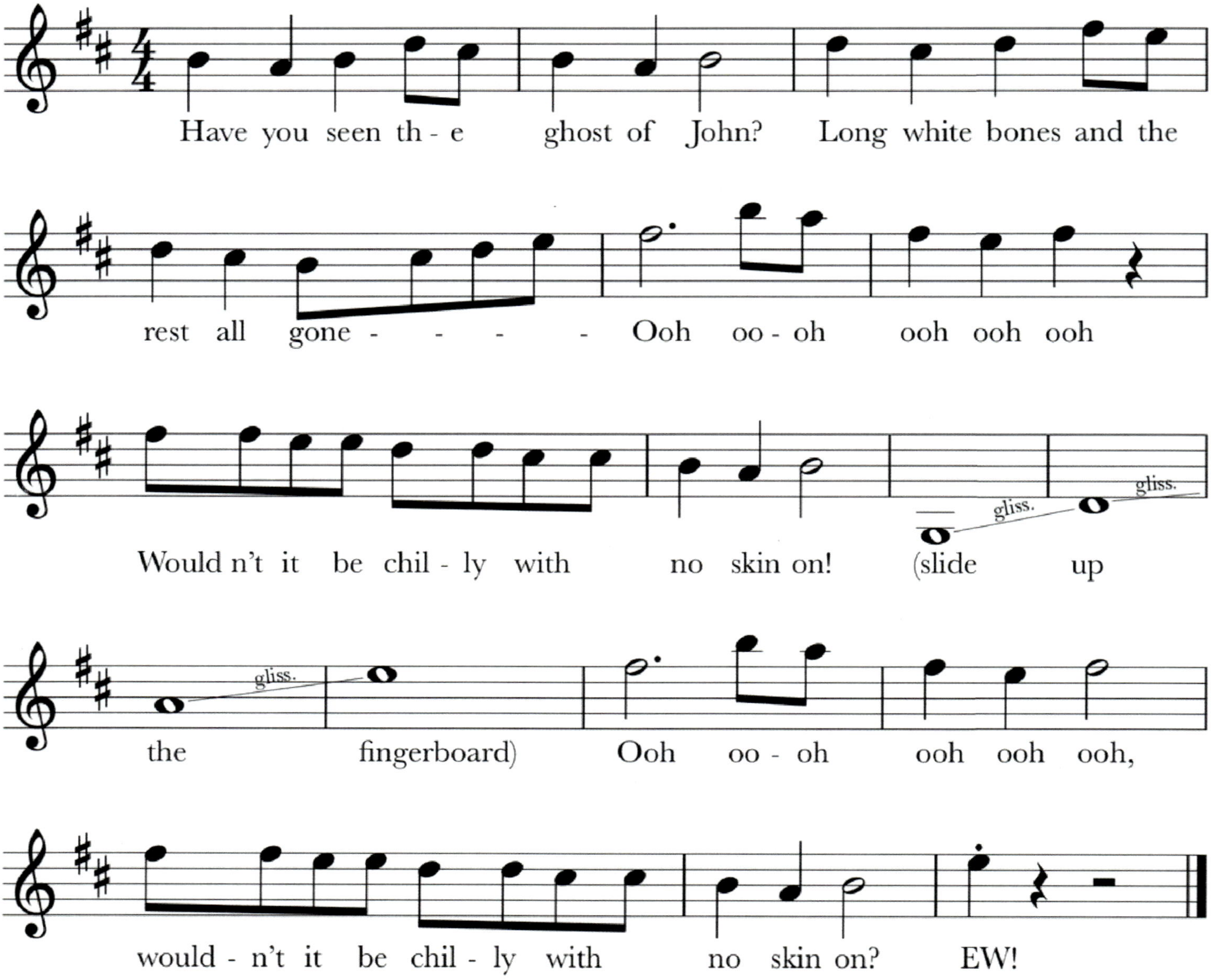

Have you seen th-e ghost of John? Long white bones and the rest all gone - - - - Ooh oo-oh ooh ooh ooh Would n't it be chil-ly with no skin on! (slide up the fingerboard) Ooh oo-oh ooh ooh ooh, would-n't it be chil-ly with no skin on? EW!

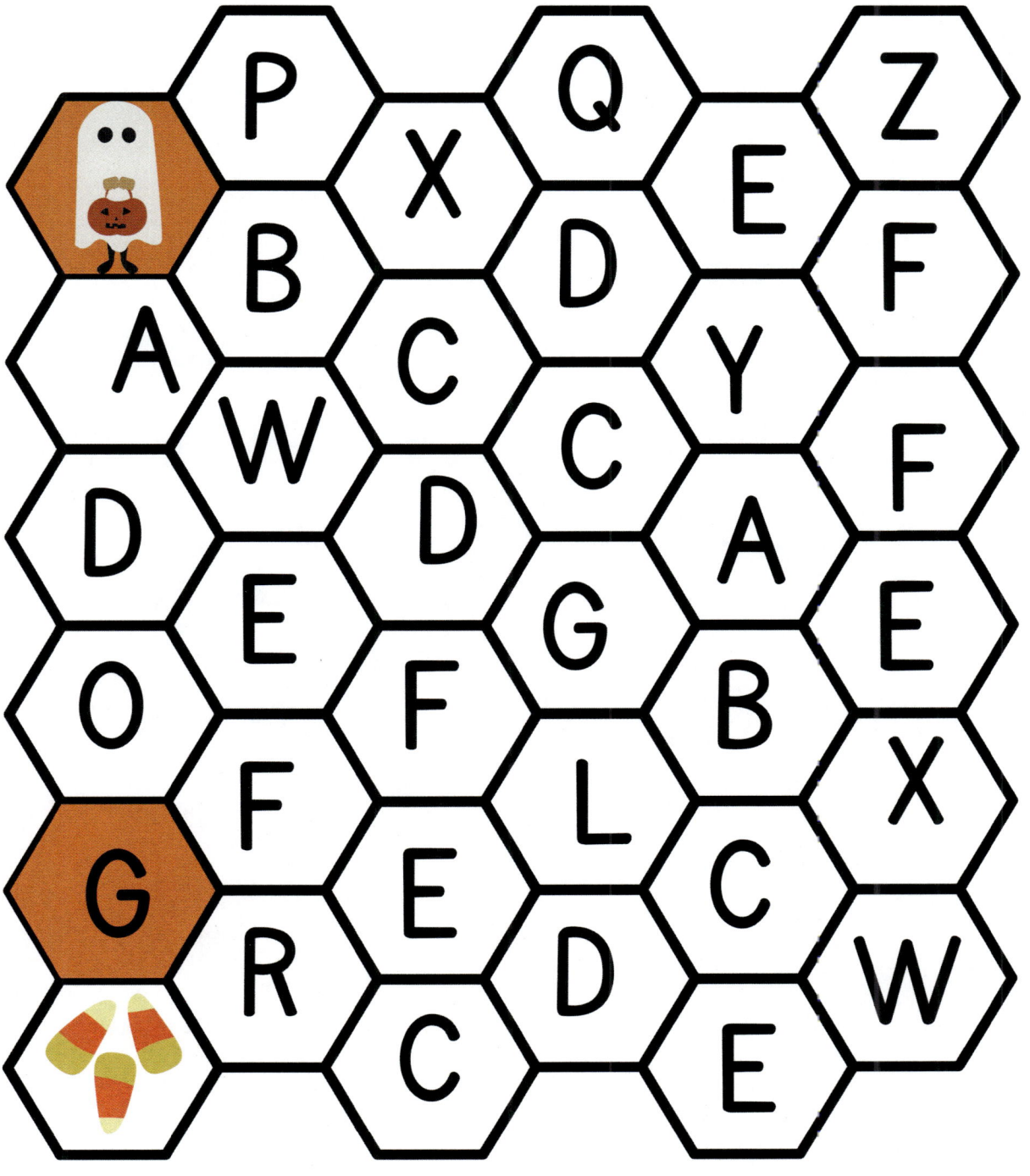

BOOK LEVEL CHART FOR THE VERY FUN VIOLIN LIBRARY

VIOLIN GRADE	FUN VIOLIN LEVEL	MAIN CONCEPTS
PRE-TWINKLE	A	RHYTHMS, FINGERS 1,2,3 ON A FINGER 1 ON E
LEVEL 1A	B	NOTE READING 1,2,3 ON A OPEN D & 1 ON E
LEVEL 1B	C	NOTE READING ON D, A & E STRINGS, FINGER 4
LEVEL 2A	D	NOTE READING ON ALL STRINGS
LEVEL 2B	E	INTRO TO 3RD POSITION & VIBRATO

C. JUDY NAILLON 2020 WWW.VIOLINJUDY.COM

CERTIFICATE
OF ACHIEVEMENT

This awarded to :

_____

for the achievement of the completion of
"A Violin Halloween"

MRS. JUDY NAILLON

"ViolinJudy"

Mrs. Judy Naillon, B.M. Violin Performance or "ViolinJudy" is a dedicated and enthusiastic independent piano and violin teacher, composer, and professional violinist. Her work consists of her large private music studio, as well as playing with her string quartet and Wichita Symphony Orchestra. She served as a church musician for over 20 years and is active in leadership in the musicians' union. She loves coming up with creative ideas to help both students and teachers be successful and blogs about it all at www.ViolinJudy.com and for Alfred's Music Publishers. When she is not writing new Violin books she loves spending time with her family and little dog Pom.

ENJOY MORE BOOKS BY AUTHOR VIOLINJUDY

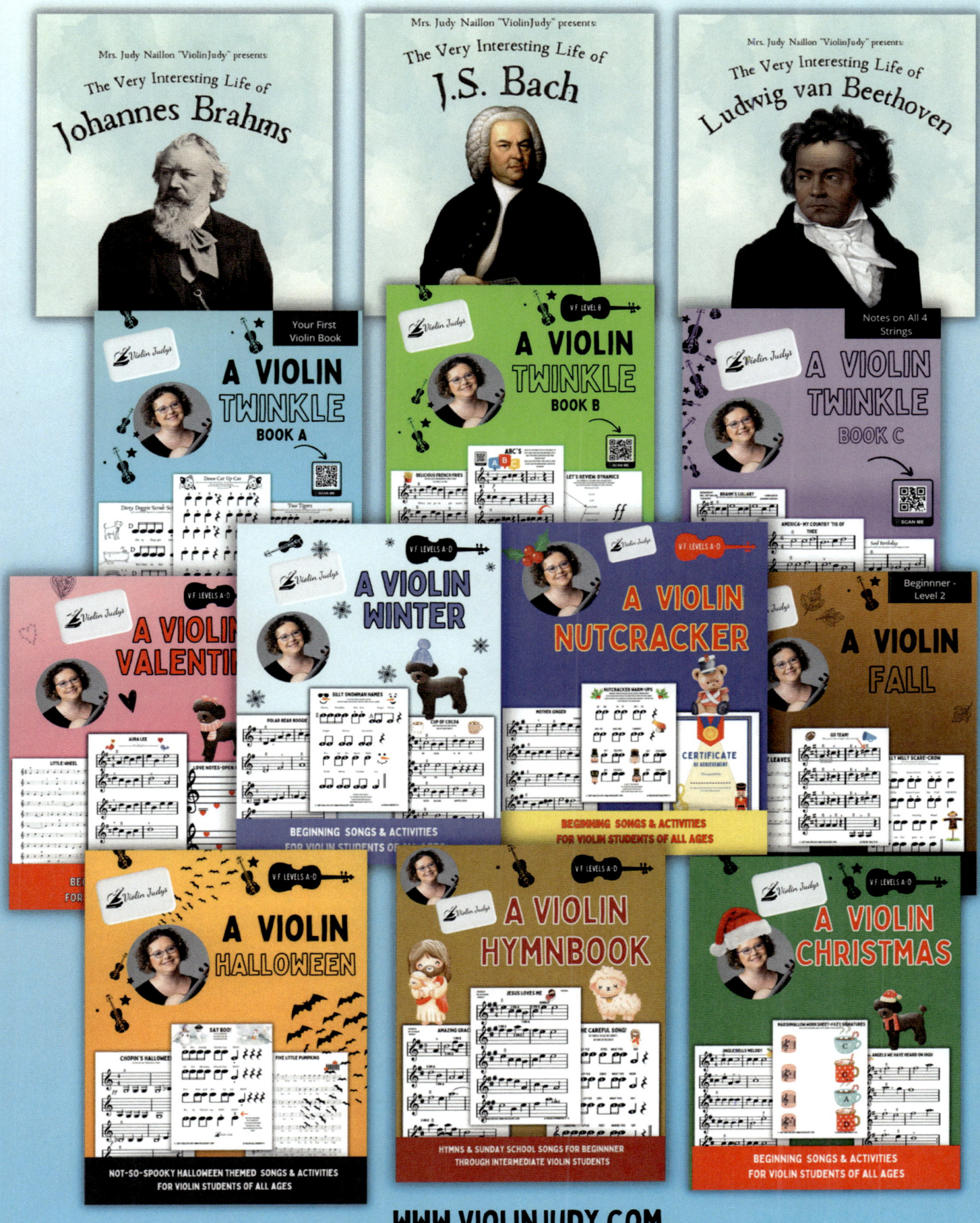

www.violinjudy.com

Made in the USA
Las Vegas, NV
06 August 2023